To Have and To Hold...

~a journey through life towards self-love~

"Because of the Lord's great Love we are not consumed, for his compassions never fail. They are new every morning; great is your faithfulness. I say to myself, The Lord is my portion; therefore I will wait for him."
Lamentations 3: 22-24

Freda Camille

To Have and To Hold
Copyright © 2017
Freda Camille

ISBN-10: 0-9912415-2-5
ISBN-13: 978-0-9912415-2-1

Published by;
Freda Camille
Chase Zion Publishing Wilmington, Delaware
http://fredacamille.com/

chasezionpublishing@gmail.com

All scripture quotations are from the New International
Version of the Bible.

Dedication

For my Mom and Dad...

Frances & Frederick Fistzgiles

I wish you were here to see the fruits of your labor, and to hear you say how proud you are of your baby girl. Miss you both. Thank you for your love and guidance. I am who I am because of you. It has been too long. Continue to rest in heaven... until we meet again!

Love always...

Acknowledgments

To my family and friends, thank you for supporting, helping and assisting me in learning to embrace myself during this journey through life and love. I am eternally grateful for your listening ears, advice and patience. Thank you for continuing to believe in me; I hold you near and dear to my heart. For you who assisted with layout design, proofreading, reviewing, editing, I ask God to continue to abundantly bless you with gifts and talents to share with the world.

I would like to express my gratitude to those who contributed to the smiles, happiness, heartache, and tears that enabled me to translate those emotions into words that fill these pages to help my readers feel understood and not alone. All relationships have peaks and valleys. It is very important for you to be sure not to lose yourself through the experience.

I would like to thank my daughter Sateyai for being my absolute inspiration. Your support and words of encouragement in this season of my life is what fuels my strength to continue to be the best mother and role model for you. My mother taught me about the true meaning of unconditional love, and I am so blessed to know her love remains alive in you. I am extremely proud of the amazing woman you are. Always remember, God has a plan for your life, and He will bring it forth! I love you baby girl!

Table of Contents

Introduction

To Have and To Hold is a poetic journey through life experiences heading towards self-love and healing from one's past. Many of these writings were inspired by an act of kindness, infatuation, or a sense of hope of what an individual may see for the future from a particular situation.

Relationships in today's society tend to lack sustenance due to the inability of deciphering love and lust. I too have sat on the side of the road of trying to figure out how to jump start the love train that has crashed and burned. Life's course takes us through so many hills and valleys, which we tend to displace our emotional instability upon others when they come into our world. Most times we ignore the signs of those who are unwilling to commit wholeheartedly. They know you are not in a position to receive what they have to offer: which usually amounts to nothing. Yet somehow, we allow ourselves to become bait to the vultures that are preying on that small bit of hope which ends up being our weakness.

We are in search of Love, not knowing that Love starts at home, inside of our own hearts. Then one day God opens our eyes, and we recognize our blessing. We begin to see that Love is patient, love is kind, it does not boast...

We understand that God created the union for us To Have and To Hold forever.

Love At First Sight

For once in my life
I think I finally believe that God has
Bestowed true love upon me.
It wasn't in a vision, although it seemed like a dream,
As I stumble over each word,
That you articulated to me,
Your wisdom much admired,
Very much different from the rest.
You captivate my mind
With your attentiveness.
Something very strange is occurring
Within my soul tonight.
Could this be an innocent case of
Love at first sight?
I could effortlessly fall into your arms
Full of faith and grace,
Anticipating empowerment and

Inspiration from your verbal embrace.

You are taking me into a realm that I

Have tried to ignore;
To prevent me from actually
Connecting emotionally anymore.
I choose to accept these feelings
I am feeling right now.
And willing to take the risk,
Whichever way this goes down.
Something very strange is occurring
Within my soul tonight.
Could this be an innocent case of
Love at first sight?

~*To Have or To Hold*~
she says:

Can I honestly look into the mirror,
and repeat these words to the
reflection that is staring back at me:
I take this woman to have and to hold
till death do us part?

I am all I have.
I mean I know
that God is always with me,
but how can I begin to accept
love from you
when I barely know how to love myself?

I am riding on the essence of my smile,
still inside I feel empty.
It is so hard for me to reciprocate
the love
that is being poured into me
because the vessel is broken.

I am trying very hard to not cast it aside
like waste...
What you are giving me is genuine...
it's authentic.
God says to love thy neighbor as thyself,
But how can I love you
when I do not love me.
It's time to get down to the truth of the matter.

My whole life has been a lie.
I have tried to live life
according to standards against my will.

My inner turmoil is getting the best of me.
I want to truly be set free
from all of the hurt and pain
by telling the truth.

My protection of others has hurt me.
How could I have allowed this to happen?
I truly am not sure of
who I am,
which in turn means
you do not know me either.

Regaining Trust

How does one begin to regain
 trust after it has been lost?
You must find your way back
to the long road of forgiveness.
After someone has hurt you,
regardless of how big or small...
You must forgive them.
Release the hurt and the pain.
This will open your heart and mind
up to be able to trust again.
I sometimes find myself
in a place where
I thought I had gotten over those hurdles in my life.
Then all of the sudden
 a familiar situation comes,
and you find that old wound has not healed.
Deliverance has not come in that area yet.
We must pray and ask God
to give us grace,
we must ask God for forgiveness,
we must forgive ourselves,
we must forgive those who have hurt us...
o that we can set ourselves free...
Now the humbling process begins.
We shall be able to trust again.

Does He Love Her?

He tells her he wants her to be happy and
says he understands,
yet how can she be happy with 3 minute phone calls,
and being at home alone with no man.
She longs for his sweet kisses & hugs,
and when her spirit is bent,
he takes time to listen and strokes her ego with
compliments.
His uplifting words she buries deep in her mind,
so she can have access to him at any given time.
then it happened, the day that she feared,
She expressed her feelings for him by releasing them
through tears.
she begins to imagine how this could be,
for he has touched spots which used to be lonely,
but now he has come and removed her pain,
reality is forever her life he has changed.
She's so in love with him, and doesn't have to worry
about a thing,
he's loosed the butterflies in her belly, and caused her
heart to sing.

Her Needs

Does a woman have to tell a man
what it is that she needs,
or should he possess a keen sense
of knowing her desires to be
pleased...
Is it her job to suggest and notion,
the ingredients that
are required in his secret love potion...
Looking into your eyes
I believe you can open me up to see,
that you can be sensitive and gentle
while handling me.
Very inquisitive I am,
to be shown how you could lead and direct,
this sensual desire to let go without losing respect.
Your poise and countenance has me twisted in my flesh,
my body screams it wants you,
wait let me put it in check.
Is this going to be a moment
that will flash right past my eyes?
and become only a memory
 that leaves me empty & asking why.
I have no expectations other than developing a bond
with my new friend.
Do you recognize that I am the answer?
Run that question by me again...

Encourage the Encourager

As each tear gently rolls down my face,
I understand that,
even the encourager
needs and desires an encouraging word.
I want off of this roller coaster...
Unfortunately,
the lesson has not been learned, and deliverance has not
been given yet,
so this ride is not over.
Can you connect with
the emotional purging from the dew that
expels from my eyes?
It is an eruption of
love, hurt, pain, and joy...
But it is up to you…
to decipher what type of medical response you
will apply
I am in need of a life line…
Are you ready to encourage me...
Can you speak life?

Strong Man

The arms of a strong man, has not held me in years;
And the touch of a real man has not wiped away my
tears.
Where is that man who can help chase away my fears,
Continually supporting and encouraging me year after
year.
If the man that God has for me walked into my life
today,
I pray I would have enough discernment to not chase
him
away.
I promise to be especially sweet as I genuinely am, I
would be uplifting and encouraging to my Godly Strong
man...
Can you look into your heart and reveal to me what you
see?
Is there a safe haven inside designed just for me?
Is there anything that you desire to take out?
Does your mind require peace and the removal of doubt,
Can we take the time to exchange love and affection?
And allow God to guide us in the right direction.
We both have had our fair share of rough times,
Together we can work to rebuild our hearts, souls, and
minds
It would not be necessary to guard our hearts so closely,
Because God orchestrated this friendship between you
and me;
Are you that strong man that my heart longs for?
The one with whom my heart could sincerely adore,
As restoration comes we can safely cross the lines,
and allow our love that is fresh and new become more
deeply defined.

Cave Man...

A 21st century Cave man has the ability to take you out
of your comfort zone...
He possesses a keen sense of being able to read between
the lines...
He recognizes a
Woman of character.
He chooses to keep his distance
& Respect her
cuz' he knows he has his own 'stuff' to figure out.
He Loves her & knocks the walls down;
causing her to Love
again...
A Cave Man gives a very well deserved experience. ♥

Has Destiny Arrived

My heart skips a beat,
and it feels like butterflies are in my belly,
I am not supposed to be feeling uneasy am I?
There was a guy that I once knew
who meant the world to me.
He was very sweet, kind, and sincere.
He treated me like
I was the most important woman in the world.
I could not imagine being without him,
Somehow our worlds went into two separate directions,
and the story ended.
Never in a million years would either of us
have ever imagined
that we'd be blessed for our worlds to collide once
again. He has not changed...
he looks the same, so handsome,
ever so gentle, and so sexy!
Oh this feeling is strange!
I am floating on air...
He admires my hair.
He smiles at me..
I am so full of glee...
this can't be real...
It seems like a dream.
It's been such a very long time
since we last laid eyes on one another...
I have to call my brother...
I think I am in shock...
God please can we stop the clock...
I don't want this moment to ever end.
I was in love with this man many years ago,
and it seems that those same exact feelings
are beginning to flow.

Is it possible that the love has been stored inside of my
heart waiting for this very day..
 the day of fate...
the moment of Destiny to arrive?
He feels the same way...
is it possible?
Could this be true?
If love is a decision,
then why are we feeling the way we do?
As if the stars in the sky have intertwined like
connect the dots.
The missing pieces to the puzzle have been found in
what was a moment in time to some...
Like a magnetic field:
two hearts have been drawn together.
He searched and I was found,
and yes history that once was has become a reality.
Now that reality has set our hearts free,
Love returns like the dove that was released from
Noah's ark...
here is so much more that God has to restore...
who believes in dreams deferred?
The one who hopes...
the one who has faith in Love...
The one who simply believes.
Yet I ask again,
If love is a decision, then what exactly is this that
I am feeling?
Are you my soul mate that my heart's been missing?
Do dreams really come true?
I can remember wishing upon a star,
and my wish was you.

History Becomes Reality

Last night as I laid in my bed,
many thoughts of you ran through my head,
suddenly out of my eyes rolled a tear,
last night I cried,
because you were not here.
I cannot understand why I feel the way that I do,
I guess it's because I have never gotten over you.

You had such an exhilarating effect on me,
I am attached and addicted to our history.
As I recollect on the special moments
we shared back then,
 I believe it was a beautiful story

 that was never supposed to end.
I am almost afraid of the way that I feel,
the mere fact that you are back in my life
seems so unreal,
Reminiscing on our love that was so true and sincere,
I can now erase all doubt and denounce the fear.
When you hold me again,
I am sure the strength in your arms has not changed,
your embrace will be full of passion,
satisfying me without shame,
Our love is no longer being held up in time,
what was previously set free has come back,
some would call it a sign.
There isn't anything more I could ask of you for me,
than for you to be the man who would love me selfishly.
just as blue is the color of the sky,
and you cannot separate the two,
Baby, I can see us together again;
I want to be the compliment of you.

Longing for Love

Do you know how it feels to long
for a sweet gentle kiss?
Awaiting your return that defines
how deeply you were missed?
Do you know how it feels to earnestly desire,
an innocent embrace engulfed
with the warmth and strength of a fire.
Could you imagine the energy
that is created by this type of Love?
For me it seemed like one that you could only dream of.
There was a time that I could not attest to its tangibility,
For I had given this love,
and it had yet to be returned to me.
I have always been enthralled with the idea of being
possessed by adoration so out of control,
One that sustains its foundation and full of sincere
passion without ever becoming cold.
Now it is you,
who has changed my perception of pure intimacy,
Creating an uninhibited atmosphere that is sensual,
captivating, and sexy.
Looking deeply into your eyes I noticed love at its peak,
Extremely attentive and prepared to define any answers
my deepest thoughts may seek.
It's so relaxing how you listen to my body's response to
determine your next move,
Opening me up to understand
why you are doing what you do.
As you take me to a special place where I have always
longed to be, no lust, shame, or perverted memory can
prevent this moment from happening to me.

Multiple runs to ecstasy,
the highest plateau has been reached,
You take your time to bring me down,
with so much more for you to teach.
I am so appreciative of you
for having such a genuine concern,
Because I was ready to walk away and
give up on this love that I have yearned.
Believing it to be an unattainable degree of passion and
desire without credibility,
but you tapped into my heart and mind
turning my dreams into reality....

~thank you~

Heart and Mind

I let precious time slip away,
not knowing God's the only one
who's here to stay.
Wasting time on things that are temporary,
yet my soul yearns for long life thru eternity.
You set a trap for me by using my past, emotionally,
I was attached and distracted; questions,
I dare not ask.
In His word it says,
in all our ways we should acknowledge Him,
and He will direct our paths.
Through prayer it was manifested to me,
that you were sent to me by the enemy,
 to kill, steal and destroy;
and hold back the gift God promised me,
God is love and His love is all that I need,
with this revelation
my heart and mind is at peace.

Heartbeat of Love

your heart...
my heart...
an everlasting beat that echoes
from our childhood...
cascades into a river that empties into a long awaited
scenery of adulthood...
it's a warm preexisting sense of love...
a beautiful experience...
slowly
becomes oblivious to life...
timeless love...
transparent love...
untouchable love...

we ♥

My Memories of Love

My heart is beating fast and
I feel as if I cannot breathe,
These feelings of anxiety are overwhelming me,
My face is so flush and I am breaking out in a sweat,
How much more inadequate could this be;
we have not even seen each other yet,
We have not had the chance to once again meet
face to face,
Nor have we had the opportunity
to occupy the same space.
So many years have passed us by continuously,
And now I've come to the realization
that I am deeply in love with a memory.
Memories of you holding me so close in your arms,
Anticipating your sweet kisses and
 how your love kept me warm,
Mesmerized by the way you would look into my eyes,
Beautiful thoughts and memories of how you have never
made me cry...
Our teenage love was young, very innocent and
immature,
And I wanted to be the only one with whom your heart
longed for,
 It takes a special kind of guy to love and appreciate his
girl,
Unfortunately we never had the chance to intermingle
our worlds,
Yet the day has come where the parallel no longer
exists,
Our paths have crossed once again and you have truly
been missed.

The memories have me so intrigued it's hard to decipher
yesterday from today, It feels so good to have you back;
I hope our friendship is here to stay.
My heart leaps and smiles with every fleeting thought I
have of you and me,
Honesty and respect were the basis of our intimacy,
I do not want to mislead you;
I don't expect your life to be rearranged,
Although our memories can become a reality;
I will always be here for you just in case anything
should change.

~Love Always

An Architect's Love

This Love God designed:
The most favorable,
the finest:
my highness,
No where you can find it,
it's Divine!
Designed for a Prince,
but made for a Queen,
Love descends from Christ the king,
so rare and fragile;
warm and pure,
once experienced you can't ignore,
it's a perfect Love that endures till no end,
A great escape that expands over any measure
to intertwine like strands of hair;
Honor Hold dear,
rich in taste without fear...

"An Architect's Love."

It is one that formulates life's endeavors,
it endures forever;
it can only get better,
It is the structure of Salvation
and the premise of Prosperity,
The Great I AM purposed it
as the foundation of our Destiny.
It inspires the hearts of men and kindles desire,
Consecration is the element that carries
Adoration much higher...

"An Architect's Love".

An Architect's Love has patience
and stretches across the horizon,
Embraces the heavens throughout the galaxy,
 Over and around, and beneath our feet.
It's deeper than the eye can see,
With respect and understanding,
He blessed you and me.
He spoke to our hearts with wisdom:
"Preserve these moments of joy and happiness,
Strongholds cannot break this bond,
no matter what the test.
Through this life,
together;
we shall walk hand in hand,
Best Friends,
She's your Lady,
And
 He is your Man...

Your Memories of Love

Your heart is beating fast,
and you feel as if you cannot breathe,
Those feeling of anxiety are overwhelming,
Your face is so flush,
and you are breaking out in a sweat,
How much more inadequate could this be;
you haven't seen each other yet,
You have not had the chance to once again
meet face to face,
nor have you had the opportunity
to occupy the same space.
So many years have passed you by continuously,
Right now you've come to the realization...
You are deep in love with a memory!

Memories of holding each other closely in your arms
anticipating sweet kisses,
and how your love was oh so warm,
Mesmerized by the way she would look into your eyes,
Beautiful thought and memories,
of how he never made your cry...
your teenage love was young,
very innocent and immature;
She wanted to be the only one with
whom your heart longed for.
It takes a special guy to love and appreciate his girl,
unfortunately you never had the chance
to intermingle your worlds.
Yet the day has come where,
the parallel no longer exists,
your paths have crossed once again,
and you have truly been missed.
The memories have you so intrigued

It's hard to decipher yesterday from today,
 it feels so good to be back,
you hope tomorrow is today.
Your heart leaps and smiles with every fleeting
thought of him.
He says he prayed every night that
he would see you again.

His Image

A man with vision and an eye to see,
A heart full of love, humble as can be.
So gifted and full of talents wealth overtakes your life,
God's the source of your existence,
in Him you take delight.
You are such a great inspiration to those around you,
Possessing creative abilities to motivate
adults and youth.
You have a dazzling smile that brightens up my day,
and the very sound of your voice takes my breath away.
I wonder if this could be the answer to silent prayers
from years ago,
or a simple glimpse at love in His image,
from where I can learn and grow;
to understand the true meaning of being loved at its best,
We adore each other's value;
it's so much different from the rest.
An attraction that has gone beyond
what the average eye can perceive,
I feel the chemistry that we have
could last throughout eternity.
Somehow we know this friendship
will stand each test that we may face,
For we know that it's in God's Image that we stand,
and ask for His saving Grace...

Her Image... You Found Me

I thank you for not making me feel like,
when we are in each other's presence...
I can't be free to be me.
It's not so important that upon each encounter,
my every strand of hair must
lie in place... perfectly,
or I must present myself as...
America's Next Top Model...
because your comprehension of a beautiful woman
far supersedes temporary man made enhancements.

You are looking to see your reflection,
the answer to your dreams and your future inside of me.
As you look into the gateway to my soul,
you begin to recognize your rib,
For God dug deep inside of man and created woman,
"Alone... no longer shall he live."
The two become one to create the perfect harmony,
The scent of our love that is released into the air –
is a Sweet melody.
I am ready for you to speak life to me,
so I can germinate the seeds
Then we can cultivate the vision that
God predestined for His Glory.
You understand your position and responsibilities
as my man;
You are patient and ever so gentle,
as your pick me right out of God's hand.

One day I will... forgive you.

I thought you were going to be different,
showing my heart no pain,
taking special care to replace and exchange the shame,
I wish I knew the ending from the very start,
I'm sure I would have
done a better job of protecting my heart,
I was under false pretenses assuming
that you were there for me,
but it was not I or my love your searched for endlessly.
How could you betray me the one you called friend?
A cross between Satan and Judas,
proclaiming true love till the end.
I never could imagine life without you and me,
but now I look at us and can't believe we're done,
Who can we blame?
Who let it go?
Was the decision fair and true?
Could all of this have happened as
a result of an insatiable you?
You did not fight long and hard
 to give our love a chance,
You willingly gave up on us to hell with romance.
Who cares about the price that it costs to raise a family;
I guess we'll just have to keep on keeping on,
in search for stability.
My heart cries out,
and I pray God keeps us comforted in his loving arms,
The battle is not lost;
the course has just changed,
May He keep us safe from harm.
I hope one day I can find the strength to honestly say
I forgive you,

because right now,
my feelings are hurt;
my heart is heavy,
and it is just so hard to do.

Suddenly you appeared

Suddenly, you appeared out of nowhere,
Like,
yesterday you were just a fantasy,
and today your composition is tangible.
You have manifested yourself to me as the one with
whom I desire to spend the rest of my life with.
I was born to be what any man would be looking to find.
Fortunately,
 I was created especially for you.
Lacking nothing;
but feeling unprepared.
It seems as if its love everlasting that you are seeking.
You walked right into me and from your heart,
I could detect this irresistible
fragrance of infatuation and adoration;
with a sprinkle of intimate communication.
You are inviting me in,
and this situation has to be one that is win-win.
What more can I ask for from you?
Your words have made a lasting impression on me.
Each sweet word has been
imprinted in my heart like a seal.
You matter and I care about what you think;
without it consuming my mind or
turning me into a robot;
I know who I am and understand my worth.
Your first impression was one that lit the eternal fire
in my soul sparked the twinkle in my eyes.
Emotions begin to flow like a Tsunami.
In an instant you change my
world like a great hurricane.

You make the difference,
and become the enhancement
to my inner and outer beauty.
You are like an added accessory
to the wardrobe that brings about completeness.
The reprimand of this connection is almost
incomprehensible in my mind,
because this Love seems...
too good to be true.
How can life have dealt such a
hand of heartache and pain;
Now the tables have turned,
and it seems I am having an
extremely hard time receiving.
I deserve this...
I begin to realize that I am being overtaken by love;
There are no walls or barriers that
I would normally put up to prevent
anyone from getting my heart can be used.
It's time to throw in the towel, because this battle here...
has been lost.
You see,
Suddenly,
 you appeared out of nowhere,
and I cease to fight anymore.
It feels peaceful and harmonious...
Truth is:
I am in Love for sure.

In Love With You

You looked at her...
she fell in love.
You spoke to her...
she fell in love.
You touched her...
she fell in love.
You held her...
so deep in love
You kissed her...
She is in love with you.

She can't see you...
she fell in love
She's crying...
she fell in love

She's confused...
so deep in love
She's hurting...
is this love?
Can't express her feelings for you.

You called her...
you fell in love
She heard you...
you fell in love
She laughed...
you fell in love
You tell her...
you are in love
She says…
I want to be with you.

To Have or To Hold: ~He~

How easy is it for me to love and motivate others,
Yet,
I yearn to master the skill in the area of tending to me.
Can I develop self-love?
Can I begin to dig into the depths of my soul and
understand that I too am special?
This love that I have for others leaves me
as an empty vessel,
Will I possess enough strength and peace to
 retain it if it's truly returned to me.
Or will I push Love aside due to my
Pride like trash or hand me downs?
Can I look at myself and repeat the phrase:
I take this Man
to have and to hold
till death do we depart...
I mean I am all I have,
Yes,
God is with me but
He wants us to Love our neighbor as we
Love ourselves...
but how am I to
 Love and take care of you if
I hate me.

Love Unavailable...

Is it possible for me to write
something sweet and poetically,
that will help you to better understand me?
Or shall I just take each moment that is given and
enable it to chance, and enjoy
every minute as if it's the very last slow dance.
Hoping our experiences can entwine and
make a path of its own, and
respond to the call to our friendship
today I woke up and
caught a glimpse of a ray of sunshine and
in an instant I realized the light was being
emitted from your smile
yesterday I was in a daze
yet it seems it's your smile today,
that I crave,
like an insatiable feeling in my heart,
or an irrational lack of the ability
to taste the flavor of fine wine sipped from a glass
or skin that it was supplied in...
it's hard not to grasp the melodic tunes
that are softly whispered into the canals of my ears,
your voice pierces the very core of my soul...
I hear your heart when you speak
I see myself in your eyes, you blink,
my heart wanes,
I exhale...
and you begin to live again;
somehow, someway, we seem to belong,
yet in a strange unplanned manner,
the connection desired is unavailable

The New Dream..

A looking glass, a vision;
Eyes open, then close without tears,
The heart has sweet intentions, to pursue the new
without fear;
A dream I had...
I saw you; no face...
 just your silhouette,
A caress and strong embrace,
was all that I could get,
No matter what yesterday said,
or what is had done before,
There are whispers from your heart that says-
tomorrow will bring so much more,
Should a storm seep its way through,
no need for us to be too concerned,
Because our Love has foreseen every issue,
together we'll be able to decipher and discern,
The best way to handle whatever comes our way,
Our hearts are spiritually connected;
fate has set the tone for us today.
The New Dream is about true love
that lasts a lifetime and eternity,
A Vision that is not only a dream,
but soon becomes our reality...

Her heart... His heart...

She whispered a message into the wind,
with hopes it would be carried into
the channels of his heart...

She's calmly & peacefully losing control and interest...
He feels secure,
but he's not paying attention...
to love,
that is evaporating into a non-existent state.

He's gonna come back...
And she...
is going to be gone!

The Moment...

I realize that every moment I spend time missing you
at that very moment you are spending time with her,
The funny thing is I don't understand why I waste my
time missing you cause,
there was a moment in time where,
she was wasting her time missing you,
And at that very moment
you were spending all of your time with me,
And I am sure there was a time that
we both was wasting time our precious time
sitting home trying to find time to spend time with you,
but you were busy out and about with someone else.
And now all the time that
I have wasted really...
is a benefit
because,
I have creatively
put my time to work
in regards to you...

It's new...

He refuses to let her in right now,
this causes her to step back and allow him
to be who God has created him to be...
In the relationship;
She has to take a few steps back and learn to trust...
Front and center is where she has been,
And now his words are being spoken and
she is taking them in,
Trying hard to not allow
what she is hearing to fall upon deaf ears,
Allowing prayer,
patience and time to build a foundation that
will last throughout the years.

Something to think about...

Falling in love for me,
has nothing to do with what one does
in a materialistic way.
It has more to do with
how one can tap into areas of my being
like no other has,
Or how one has the ability to alter
my current perception
or view on life and love.
Causing me to make the decision
to allow myself to feel, believe, and receive emotion;
I appreciate the responsiveness and admiration
being shown by you,
The constant reminders and attention
without conditions blow my mind,
I look forward to each days encounter with you,
because it defies every negative experience
I've partaken in.
Just the sound of your voice
takes me to a place of solitary,
A serene and intimate place that only you possess
the wherewithal to read through the complexity,
You are the missing piece to the puzzle,
our hearts are craving more,
We both deserve God's very best,
Our kisses are electrifying,
releasing a sweet fragrance
incomparable to anything we've ever sensed,
the intensity in our embrace is exhausting,
it slowly takes our breath away,
however the spark in our eyes restores our energy, and
we begin to absorb

36

the dew of love
that is being released from our skin.
Mentally we have become one,
our hearts are now smiling and connected,
We now wait for life
to set the tone and lead us in the right direction...

... now baby that,
 is something to think about

My love....

My love for you has not changed.
But your love for me has,
it has grown and matured.
You have come to an understanding
that love is not about getting
it is about giving and
putting someone before your needs and wants.
You are growing and learning
to no longer be on the side of receiving.
You understand what friendship is about.

The Day Love Left...

The day love left,
you evaluated so many things,
Like,
what was it that
"I did wrong to make you leave?
I thought we were meant to be!
I know you had love for me, and I had love for you...
But it seems as if that was not enough to keep us.
So,
now I am missing you so very much.
It was an experience that we had not had before.
The problem is your issue with trust,
my issue with trust...
Were you honest?
Was I honest?
I thought I knew everything about you,
so I prejudged you,
I was afraid of love and being hurt by you,
With all of the confidence I possessed,
I still did not believe
 I could be loved without being manipulated by:
hidden agendas. I knew I wasn't ready,
and maybe you weren't either;
The day love left,
you evaluated so many things,
It left,
because it had unfinished business elsewhere...
"Consequently,
I did not trust you."

Two Heartbeats...

Two Heart Beats,
They have a connection,
The rhythms sync like an artist
Singing on a track..
Created by the producer
who is the mastermind behind the single being on wax;
as we gaze into each other's eyes,
it's like,
depositing a quarter into the juke box of our souls;
Our blood begins to flow to a smooth tempo,
So,
 we move our feet and bodies
To the melodies,
Fate has been whispering (singing)
Into the atmosphere since we were teens...
Powerless we are,
Unable to resist and hold back,
The desire to embrace,
To kiss...
to love...
Two Heart Beats,
Intune,
Synchronized...
Destined to Be...
One...

Poetry Muse...

Today I wrote a poem,
while I sat quietly thinking about you,
In silence
I was reminded of so many things we used to do
Laugh, joke, talk, and, smile...
Sometimes,
you 'd get mad at me as well...
But, the fact that you could trust me,
was the most important detail...
Trust me with your heart,
Trust me with your mind,
Trust me with your feelings,
Trust me with your time...
It did not matter the hour,
It did not matter the day,
It did not even matter
what words that your heart had to say...
Today,
I wrote a poem,
while I sat quietly thinking about you,
In silence,
I was reminded my poetry misses it's muse...

Have you...

Have you ever kissed
your man's soul with words of peace,
Embraced him with thoughts of joy,
 touched him with hands that heal wounds of his past,
Have you ever enabled your man by caressing his ideas,
Spoke tender words into his imagination,
understood his purpose,
to help bring life to his dreams and visions,
Have you ever listened
to the stillness or your togetherness,
basked in the scent of his presence,
and appreciated his existence...
of his total being...
your Man...
Have you?

Rules of Love...

Dear Love,
I have been told that you are not a game,
Yet there are so many rules to play by,
Like, never chase...
be chased,
Don't care,
be called not the caller;
Don't ever say I love you first...
~and never let `em see you sweat;
But Love...
I want to call because I do care...
As a matter of fact,
 I Love you deep down to the core of my soul...
I've loved you before we met,
Like you and I were meant to be;
Your voice penetrates the layers of my skin,
and sends signals to the vertebral cortex in my spine.
Sometimes,
I can't even look into your eyes 'cause Love,
I know that you will decode my thought process,
within every blink...
and every moment of communication
with you triggers a jolt of life,
like a rescue inhaler elongating breaths...
so Love,
I am just going to take
pleasure in every facet and substance of you,
Without overthinking and having reservations,
Love, I let go...
God is Love...
It is time that I trust...
You.

The Aroma...

The aroma he left,
in the stairwell
A scent that I can...
still smell...
is left inside of my nose,
Like an embrace from the one with whom,
You'd never let go...
Stagnant, yet graceful...
It's fumes,
I can taste,
Almost like a kiss,
Before you exit a room,
Upon my cheek you'd place.
Remaining there for a moment...
-dazed, I walk away with good thoughts,
yet many I will not tell...
So inspired and engulfed,
by the aroma he left in the stairwell.

Do you think about me...

I go to bed wondering if:
You are thinking about me;
are you missing me?
Then I fall asleep and there you are in my dreams!
You show up and show out;
I enjoy the way love feels,
Only for me to wake up and find out;
it was simply a dream and it was not real.
I go throughout my day wondering:
if you are thinking about me, are you missing me?
Can't wait to return to bed to see you in my dreams...

Our Synergy... Kinetic Energy

Your strength draws and tugs at the greatness
deep with inside of me,
Like a magnetic force,
all that which is out of balance,
desires to line up with your synergy,
My weaknesses match your areas of power,
My strengths fuels your intellectual and spiritual nature.
Your innovative skills and gifts impressively
compliment my creative abilities and talents,
The interpretation of our love is a perfectly penned
stanza from a collection of romantic poetry.
The benefit of each moment spent with you
rewards a mood of a first date;
Consistent breathtaking experiences that
never escapes the mind,
Encounters archived to be relived again and again;
I adore how we inhale each other's intelligence,
And exhale confidence with respect and appreciation.
Safe and Secure with you,
Baby you make me better,
I look into your eyes and see,
Our Synergy is like Kinetic Energy,
You've become my best friend...
So in love with the Man you are
Praying our love story transcends.

untitled...

what is it about a man that drives a woman so wild,

make her step up her game and revolutionize her

style, cause her to feel so important and beautiful

inside, always knowing the right words to say

which makes her grin and smile.

when her esteem has been lowered

to the point of no return,

the first man who comes and fills the void

can appear to give the love

she yearns,

looking into his eyes she sees feelings of lust,

but misinterprets it as love,

now she unlocks the gate of trust,

now opening herself into believing that

he is interested in her every being,

she's blinded by what she thinks is love

cause the disguise

he's wearing can't be seen.

But what exactly is it about you that

makes me feel so out of control,

I have already played the game so

I know that there is a goal,

what exactly is the intent of me falling for you,

it may be to get you to do those things that

I desire for my man to do,

like spend a little time and live each moment

as if it were our last,

appreciate me, respect me, enjoy me

now all I do is think about you,

wanting to hear you call me baby and

say that I am your boo,

remind me of all the things

you desire for us to experience,

I aspire to see you so I can escape into your eyes,

as you admire my beauty,

I throw an extra switch into my stride.

the visualization is not enough,

what you see is tantalizing and enticing you

compelling you to control the feelings

of wanting to taste this forbidden fruit.

we are getting closer and closer to crossing the line,

every time I envision you

erotic thoughts run through my mind.

the fantasies are deep,

I can't understand why I feel the way I do

It's some kind of special vibe that

I am getting from you.

I am not the type of lady that jumps at the first chance,

but I knew that you were different

upon my initial glance;

you are mysterious, so sweet, gentle and kind,

In my heart I feel that you are a great find.

What is it that you are doing to me?

I feel beautiful and sexy, I want to be free;

to be caressed and embraced in your strong arms,

with you I feel protected from all danger and harm,

I don't know how much longer

I can keep these feelings inside,

the way I feel about you

should not come to you as a surprise.

My heart flutters, and then it skips a beat,

a battle once won, now ends with defeat.

there will always be a secret place

within my heart locked

for you my friend,

make sure you keep the key cause

I never want this to end.